About the Author™

Meet
J. K. Rowling

S. Ward

The Rosen Publishing Group's
PowerKids Press™
New York

Published in 2001, 2003 by The Rosen Publishing Group, Inc.
29 East 21st Street, New York, NY 10010

Revised Edition 2003

Book Design: Maria Melendez

Photo Credits: Cover, title page, (portrait of J. K. Rowling), p. 4 (portrait of J. K. Rowling) © Mitch Gerber/CORBIS; p. 6 (Church Cottage, Tutshill), p. 7 (Forest of Dean), p. 8 (University of Exeter) photo courtesy of the University of Exeter, England; p. 10 (Edinburgh Castle) © Dave G. Houser/CORBIS; p. 11 © Associated Press AP/Suzanne Mapes; p. 12 (Nicolsons Restaurant) photo courtesy of Nicolsons Restaurant, Edinburgh; pp. 16, 22 Everett Collection; p. 19 (book-signing session by J. K. Rowling) © AP/Wide World Photos; p. 18 (Tutshill Primary School).

Grateful acknowledgment is made for permission to reprint previously published material on pp. 5, 9, 13, 14, 15, 17, and 20: book cover and text excerpts on pp. 131 and 189 From HARRY POTTER AND THE SORCERER'S STONE by J. K. Rowling. Text copyright © 1997 by J. K. Rowling, illustration copyright © 1998 by Mary GrandPré. Published by Arthur Levine Books, an imprint of Scholastic Press. Reprinted by permission of Scholastic Inc.; book cover and text excerpts on pp. 22 and 207 From HARRY POTTER AND THE CHAMBER OF SECRETS by J. K. Rowling. Text copyright © 1999 by J. K. Rowling, illustration copyright © 1999 by Mary GrandPré. Published by Arthur Levine Books, an imprint of Scholastic Press. Reprinted by permission of Scholastic Inc.; text excerpt on p. 334 From HARRY POTTER AND THE PRISONER OF AZKABAN by J. K. Rowling. Text copyright © 1999 by J. K. Rowling, illustration copyright © 1999 by Mary GrandPré. Published by Arthur Levine Books, an imprint of Scholastic Press. Reprinted by permission of Scholastic Inc.

Ward, S. (Stasia), 1968–
    Meet J. K. Rowling / S. Ward.—1st ed.
  p. cm. — (About the author)
    Summary: An easy-to-read biography of J. K. Rowling, the English author of the popular Harry Potter series of children's books.
  ISBN 0-8239-6808-1 (alk. paper)
  1. Rowling, J. K.—Juvenile literature. 2. Authors, English—20th century—Biography—Juvenile literature. 3. Children's stories—Authorship—Juvenile literature. [1. Rowling, J. K. 2. Authors, English. 3. Women—Biography.] I. Title. II. Series.

PR6068.O93 Z9 2000
823'.914—dc21
[B]   00-025375

Manufactured in the United States of America

Contents

Harry Potter

In 1997, a book called *Harry Potter and the Philosopher's Stone* arrived in bookstores in England. The story was about an 11-year-old orphan named Harry Potter. An orphan is a child who no longer has parents. Harry finds out that he is a **wizard**. Children and grown-ups loved reading about Harry Potter. The book became a **best-seller**.

In 1998, the book was printed in the United States. The title was changed to *Harry Potter and the Sorcerer's Stone*. It became a hit in the United States, too. The **author** of the book is J. K. Rowling. The story of how she wrote it is as amazing as that of Harry Potter himself.

◀ J. K. Rowling wrote a book about Harry Potter, a young orphan who finds out that he has magical powers. The book became a best-seller.

"It happened again. It was as though the broom was trying to buck him off. But Nimbus Two Thousands did not suddenly decide to buck their riders off. Harry tried to turn back toward the Gryffindor goal posts . . . and then he realized that his broom was completely out of his control."

—from p. 189 of *Harry Potter and the Sorcerer's Stone* (1997)

Childhood

Joanne Kathleen Rowling grew up in a place called Forest of Dean, England. Her father was a factory manager. Her mother was a lab **technician**. Joanne and her sister, Di, went to Tutshill Primary School and later to Wyedean Comprehensive School. This is a state-run day school like the public schools in the United States. Joanne did well in school. Her great dream was to become a writer. She wrote her first story at the age of six. The story was called "Rabbit." Joanne loved to read. One of her favorite books as a child was *The Little White Horse* by Elizabeth Goudge. Later, she read the *Chronicles of Narnia* by C. S. Lewis.

Joanne lived in this church cottage in Tutshill Village in Forest of Dean

Joanne was born on July 31, 1965, in Bristol, England. She grew up in the Forest of Dean (right), which is a national forest park in southwestern England. ▶

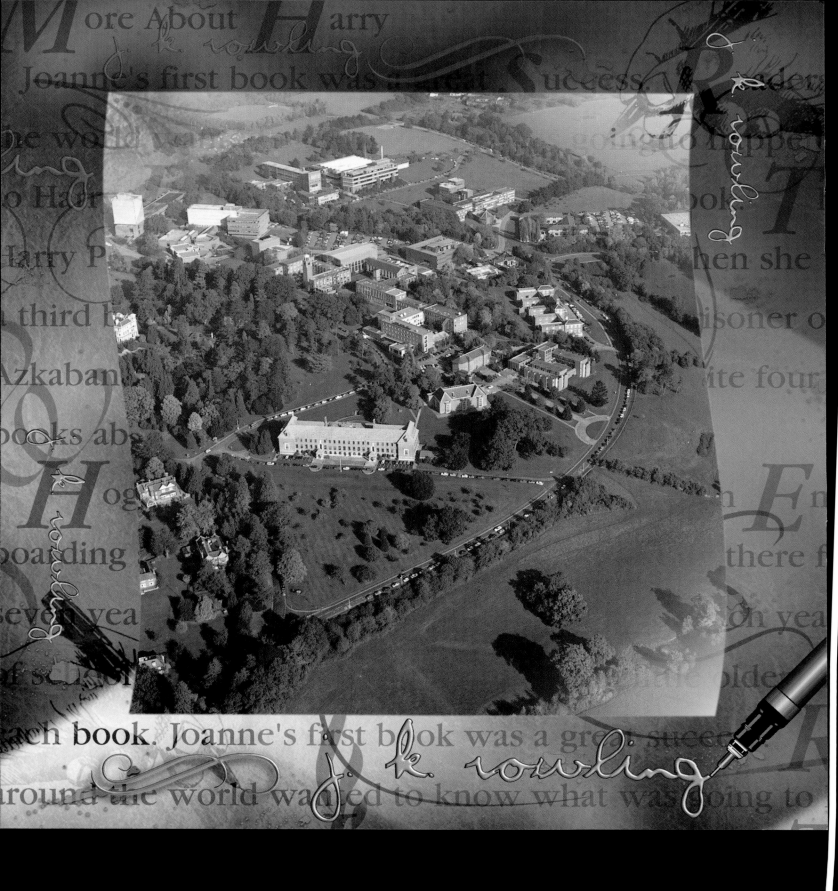

An Idea for a Story

Joanne studied French at the University of Exeter in England. Her parents hoped she could get work as a **bilingual** secretary. This was not what Joanne really wanted to do.

One day in 1990, Joanne was traveling on a train from Manchester to London in England. She was staring out the window when an idea for a story came into her mind. She imagined a boy who was trying to find his identity. In other words, he was trying to find out who he really was. This was the beginning of the **character** Harry Potter.

◄ The University of Exeter is located in the city of Exeter, in southwestern England. Joanne studied French at the University of Exeter and planned to become a bilingual secretary.

"Harry yelled in shock and backed away into the desk. . . . the bird, meanwhile, had become a fireball; it gave one loud shriek and next second there was nothing but a smouldering pile of ash on the floor."

—from p. 207 of *Harry Potter and the Chamber of Secrets* (1999)

Tough Times

Having an idea for a good story did not make life easy for Joanne. Her mother died soon after Joanne started to write about Harry. Then Joanne lost her job.

In September 1990, she traveled to Portugal to take a job teaching English. She met a Portuguese journalist. A journalist gathers, writes, and presents news for a newspaper or magazine. The two fell in love and got married. They had a daughter, Jessica. The marriage was not a happy one. Joanne got **divorced**. She was on her own in a **foreign** country with a baby. She decided to go to Edinburgh, Scotland, to be near her sister, Di.

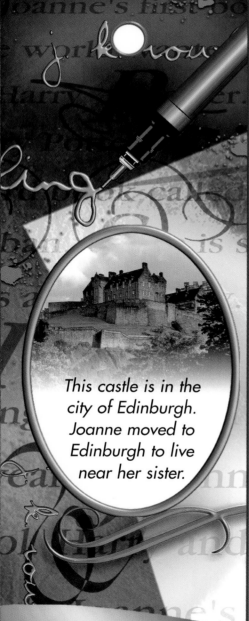

This castle is in the city of Edinburgh. Joanne moved to Edinburgh to live near her sister.

The early 1990s were difficult years for Joanne. With the printing of her first book just around the corner, though, she would soon become a worldwide success. ▶

10

Harry Potter

Struggling Writer

By the time Joanne moved to Edinburgh she had already written three chapters of the first Harry Potter book. Joanne did not have a job in Edinburgh. She did not have enough money to live on. Joanne got some **public assistance** but she could not get childcare for Jessica. There was no way she could work without having someplace to leave her daughter.

Joanne often escaped from her tiny apartment. Joanne would put Jessica in a stroller and go to Nicolsons Café, which was her favorite **café**. Joanne wrote parts of the Harry Potter book while Jessica napped in the stroller.

Cheery Nicolsons Café in Edinburgh (see map) was a place where Joanne wrote parts of Harry Potter's story in 1994. This photo of the café shows it after it was fixed up in 1999.

"There were a hundred and forty-two staircases at Hogwarts: wide, sweeping ones; narrow, rickety ones; some that led somewhere different on a Friday; some with a vanishing step halfway up that you had to remember to jump."

—from p. 131 of Harry Potter and the Sorcerer's Stone (1997)

13

Published!

> *"What was the good of magicking himself out of his room if Hogwarts would expel him for doing it? Yet life at Privet Drive had reached an all-time low. Now that the Dursleys knew they weren't going to wake up as fruit bats, he had lost his only weapon."*
>
> —from p. 22 of *Harry Potter and the Chamber of Secrets* (1999)

It took Joanne five years to finish writing *Harry Potter and the Sorcerer's Stone*. When it was done, she did not have enough money to make photocopies. She had to type two copies of the story. She knew she would need to send one copy out to a **publisher**. She kept the second copy. Joanne looked in a writer's **directory** and found an **agent** named Christopher Little. Christopher helped Joanne find a publisher for her story. In 1995, Bloomsbury Press bought Joanne's book. One of the best moments of Joanne's life was when she found out that her book was going to be **published**.

Mary GrandPré is the illustrator of Joanne's first book, Harry Potter and the Sorcerer's Stone. *Joanne thought it was a dream come true when the book was published.*

J. K. Rowling

More About Harry

Joanne's first book was a great success. Readers around the world wanted to know what was going to happen next to Harry Potter. Joanne wrote three more books. They are called *Harry Potter and the Chamber of Secrets*, *Harry Potter and the Prisoner of Azkaban*, and *Harry Potter and the Goblet of Fire*. She plans to write three more books about Harry.

Harry goes to school at Hogwarts. This is a magical school that is like an English **boarding school**. He will study there for seven years. Joanne will write a book for each year of school. Harry and his friends will get a little older in each book.

Joanne's first book, Harry Potter and the Sorcerer's Stone, *was made into a movie in 2001. The movie's characters Ron Weasley, Harry Potter, and Hermione Granger are seen here at Hogwarts.*

"Harry reached for his wand, but too late—the dog had made an enormous leap and the front paws hit him on the chest; he keeled over backward in a whirl of hair; he felt its hot breath, saw inch-long teeth—"

—from p. 334 of *Harry Potter and the Prisoner of Azkaban* (1999)

A World of Fans

Joanne writes her books in what is known as British English. Some of the words used in the British books might be confusing to American readers. In the United States, Joanne's books are published by Scholastic Press. Joanne's American **editor** is named Arthur Levine. Arthur helps Joanne change the British words into words that American readers will understand better.

British and American readers are not the only ones who love Harry Potter. Harry has fans around the world. The Harry Potter books have been **translated** into 28 languages, including Icelandic and Croatian.

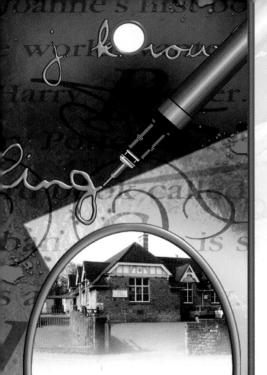

The Tutshill Primary School, where Joanne went to school.

In October 1999, crowds of fans lined up to ask Joanne to sign copies of the Harry Potter books. "Potter Mania," or the Harry Potter craze, affected the whole world. ▶

More About Harry

Joanne's first book was a great success. ... the world wanted to know what was going to happen to Harry Potter. Joanne wrote another book ... then she ... third book ... isoner of ... zkaban. ... te four ... ooks about ... Hogw ... oarding school. In the books, Harry will study there for ... even years. Joanne will write one story for each year ... f school. Harry and his friends will get a little older ... ach book. Joanne's first book was a great success ... round the world wanted to know what was going to ...

Characters

In the Harry Potter books, Harry has a friend named Hermione Granger. Hermione always wants to do very well in school. Joanne says she made Hermione a lot like herself at age 11, only smarter. Harry is a little like Joanne, too. Like Joanne, Harry is sad that his mom died.

There are four other important characters in the Harry Potter books. Harry's best friend is Ron Weasley. Hagrid is a giant who cares for the strange animals at Hogwarts School. Professor Dumbledore is the head of Hogwarts. Voldemort is the evil wizard who killed Harry's parents.

Wizard Words:
Muggle—A person who is not magical.
Parselmouth—A wizard who can talk to snakes.
Quidditch—A wizard sport that is played on broomsticks.

Wizard Places:
Diagon Alley—A street full of magical shops.
Gringotts—A wizard bank deep under the streets of London that is run by goblins.
Hogsmeade—An all-wizard village.

In Harry Potter and the Chamber of Secrets, *Harry and his friends Ginny and Ron Weasley try to stay one step ahead of trouble at the magical school.*

Keep on Writing

The year 2001 was an exciting one for Joanne. In March, Queen Elizabeth II awarded an Order of the British Empire, a medal of achievement, to Joanne for her work in children's literature. In November, Joanne bought a home in Perthshire, Scotland. Also in November, her first book was made into a movie. *Harry Potter and the Sorcerer's Stone* ended 2001 as the top moneymaking movie of the year. On December 26, Joanne married Dr. Neil Murray.

Today Joanne continues to write about Harry Potter's adventures. She believes that she might feel sad when she finishes writing the Harry Potter books. The good news is that even after Harry, Joanne will keep on writing!

Daniel Radcliffe (Harry) in Harry Potter and the Chamber of Secrets.

22

Glossary

agent (AY-jent) A person who helps a writer, actor, or athlete with his or her career.

author (AW-thur) A person who writes books, articles, or reports.

best-seller (BEST-SEH-lur) A book that sells more copies than any other book during a certain period of time.

bilingual (by-LIN-gwel) A person who speaks two languages.

boarding school (BOR-ding SKOOL) A school where students live during the school year.

café (kah-FAY) A coffee shop or restaurant.

character (KAR-ek-tur) A person or animal that appears in a story.

directory (dih-REK-teh-ree) A book or list of names and addresses.

divorced (dih-VORST) When a married couple has legally ended their marriage.

editor (EH-dih-ter) The person in charge of correcting errors, checking facts, and deciding what will be printed in a newspaper, book, or magazine.

foreign (FOR-in) Outside one's own country.

public assistance (PUH-blik uh-SIS-tens) Money given by the government to help people who do not have enough to live on.

published (PUH-blishd) Something that is printed for people to read.

publisher (PUH-blish-uhr) A person or company whose business is printing and selling books.

technician (tek-NISH-en) A person who knows the special details and methods of a subject or job.

translated (trans-LAYT-ed) Changed from one language into another.

wizard (WIH-zerd) A person with magical powers.

Index

Web Sites

Due to the changing nature of Internet links, PowerKids Press has developed an online list of Web sites related to the subject of this book. This site is updated regularly. Please use this link to access the list: www.powerkidslinks.com/aa/jkrowl/